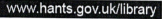

W S on turtles?

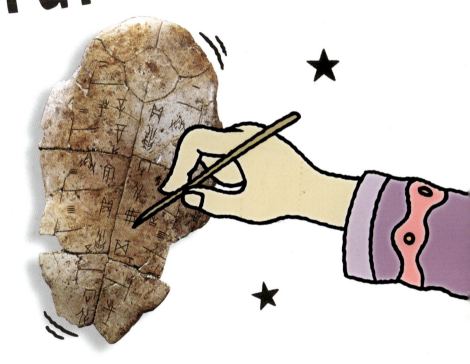

and other questions about the SHANG DYNASTY

Tim Cooke

First published in Great Britain in 2021
by Wayland

© Hodder and Stoughton, 2021

Credits:
Editor: Julia Bird
Design and illustrations: Matt Lilly
Cover design: Matt Lilly

ISBN hb 9781526315366
ISBN pb 9781526315373

Printed and bound in Hong Kong

MIX
Paper from
responsible sources
FSC® C104740

FSC
www.fsc.org

Picture credits:

Alamy: Album 12; China Images 6l; Granger Historical Picture Archive 1, 11c; Anton Hazewinkel 28b; Historic Illustrations 26b; Historic Images 20c; Peter Horree 10b; Imagine China 14bl, 16; The Picture Art Collection 23b; Xinhua 14.
Dreamstime: Beibaoke1 17; Jochenschneider 24cr.
Metropolitan Museum of Art, New York: PD/Bequest of Addie W Khan,1949: 29t.
Shutterstock: Adult24 4bl; Anusin 4br; David Carillet 18b; Kittiwat Chaitoep 27; Hung Chung Chi 5t; Chuyuss 14bc; Diogoppr 6r; Gazlast 8t; Guo Zhong Hua 21b; Fuyu Liu 26t; Maeadv 15b; W Scott McGill 25t; MXW Stock 24c; Nattanan726 29b; NattapolStudi0 20-21t; Shan_shan 15t, 20b, 22b; Silver Spiral Arts 14c; Spainic 7t; Sripfoto 18c; Vadimmmus front cover c; Vvoe 14cr, 24cl; Yellow Cat 24b; Yxm2008 23t.

Wayland
An imprint of
Hachette Children's Group
Part of Hodder and Stoughton
Carmelite House
50 Victoria Embankment
London EC4Y 0DZ

An Hachette UK Company
www.hachette.co.uk
www.hachettechildrens.co.uk

Contents

Who were the Shang?

The Shang were the first Chinese dynasty. Well, that's what most historians think anyway. A dynasty is a series of rulers who all come from the same family.

Famous dynasty

Other peoples had lived in what is now China for centuries before the Shang. However, the Shang were the first people that we know anything definite about.

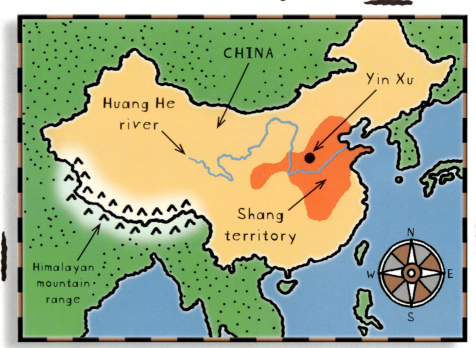

The Shang ruled an area in the North China Plain, around the Huang He river. Their reign lasted from about 1600 to 1050 BCE*. During that time, they had a number of capital cities. The last Shang capital was at Yin Xu (now Anyang).

* **BCE** stands for **B**efore the **C**ommon **E**ra, which began in the year 0. So the Shang Dynasty began over 3,500 years ago!

In just under 500 years, the Shang laid the foundations for a lot of China's history, including:

- ancestor worship
- crop farming
- jade carving
- and Chinese writing.

Rice

AM I A TORTOISE OR A TURTLE?

A bronze vessel

As well as...

- divination
- silk-weaving
- astronomy
- metalworking
- warfare
- the Great Wall of China.

Not just a legend

For a long time, historians believed stories about the Shang were exaggerated. There was no record that the dynasty had ever existed. Historians thought they belonged to legend, like other Chinese dynasties.

WRONG!

In the 20th century the first real evidence of the Shang's existence was found. Since then, archaeologists have found all kinds of traces of the Shang. There is **writing on turtle shells** and animal bones. There are tombs that contain huge bronze vessels. There are pieces of carved jade, ivory and bone. There are war chariots and jewellery.

It turns out that there is lots of evidence about the Shang, and lots about them that we still have to learn.

The best way to learn is to keep asking questions. So ask away!

Shang dynasty jewellery

Why did the Shang love AND hate mud?

The Shang lived in the valley of the Huang He, which means the Yellow River. What colour do you think the water was? [Hint: the clue is in the name!]

I'M MELLOW YELLOW!

Yellow River (Huang He)

Muddy waters

The water was full of yellow-brown silt, or mud, that the river carried from high up in the mountains of western China. When the river flooded, the silt covered the fields along the riverbanks. The silt was full of nutrients. It created the perfect soil for growing crops.

Shang farmers loved the river mud. That meant the king loved it, too. He owned all the land in the kingdom, including all the farms. All the farmers worked for him.

Shang king

I REALLY DO LOVE MUD!

Most of the farmers were poor and had hard lives. In return for working on the king's farms, they got somewhere to live and food to eat.

What was on a Shang menu?

Not much, really. **FISH** and **MEAT**, if you were rich (but you probably weren't). Most people ate a lot of **GRAINS**. That means millet, barley, rice and wheat. But mainly millet.

Shang porridge

The Shang ground millet into flour. Most often, the flour was boiled with water to make a soupy mixture called congee, which was a bit like porridge.

Marvellous millet

Millet is a grass that produces lots of grain. People still eat it in many parts of the world, particularly in Africa and Asia.

Millet grains

I WISH SYRUP HAD BEEN INVENTED...

Not so marvellous mud

The same floods that covered the fields with mud did LOTS of damage. The Huang He flooded often, but unpredictably. So many people drowned that the river earned a new nickname: China's Sorrow.

The Shang tried to tame the river. They built huge banks called levees to contain the water in the river channel.

Levees

Guess what they built the banks from? That's right: more mud.

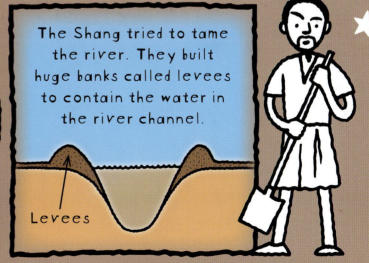

Who was the Shang's favourite ruler?

If you lived under the Shang, the best answer was probably: 'Whoever's on the throne right now'.

(Shang kings could be ruthless. You wouldn't want to offend them!)

No women allowed

All the Shang rulers were kings, by the way. One of the king's jobs was talking to the gods. The Shang believed the gods wouldn't listen to a woman, so there was never a female Shang leader.

Tang of Shang

Over 600 years, the Shang had 30 kings. Cheng Tang was the founder of the Shang dynasty, and is usually seen as their best king.

MY PEOPLE ADORE ME!

Cheng Tang seized power from a people called the Xia, who had ruled the Shang and their neighbours for over 400 years.

WE LOVE TANG!

WE LOVE CHENG!

CHENG TANG!

TANGTASTIC!

CHENG TANG FOREVER

TANG'S OUR MAN!

A terrible king …

The last Xia king, Jie, on the other hand was useless. He treated his people with great cruelty and forced them to build him lavish palaces. Meanwhile, he literally lived like a king.

MY PEOPLE HATE ME!

In about 1600 BCE Cheng Tang persuaded Jie's subjects to rise up against him. Cheng Tang raised an army and defeated Jie at the Battle of Mingtiao. Jie fled into exile.

WE HATE JIE! WE HATE JIE!

JIE OUT!

DOWN WITH JIE!

TIME TO FLEE JIE!

… And a better version

Cheng Tang became the first Shang king after the battle. In contrast with Jie, he tried to help his people. He cut taxes and did not force men to serve in his army.

The Mandate of Heaven

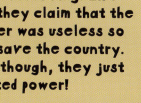

Cheng Tang said he took power under the Mandate of Heaven. That means the gods gave him the authority to rule the country.

Many Chinese rulers have used this idea to justify taking power from the previous king. Like Cheng Tang, they claim that the previous ruler was useless so they had to save the country. Sometimes, though, they just wanted power!

Why did the Shang write on turtles?

HUMPHH!

DEAR SHANGDI

The Shang often scratched questions on the undershells of turtles. The shells were flat to write on, and the Shang had lots of turtles. (Poor turtles!)

Supreme Shangdi

The questions were addressed to Shangdi, the Shang's supreme ancestor. The Shang believed that, long ago, Shangdi had created the first Shang people. Now he lived as a god. The Shang believed Shangdi watched over them. They asked his opinion on nearly everything.

These were some of the things the Shang asked about:

Shangdi

The weather

The right time to plant crops

Keeping the king in good health

The likely result of a battle

The right way to perform rituals

They even asked questions about how to **ASK** Shangdi questions! (like: Are we doing this right?!)

Shangdi was so important that any random Shang couldn't ask him a question. All questions came through the priests, led by the king. Unfortunately, Shangdi never gave a simple answer.

Well, you could hardly expect a god-ancestor to speak like an ordinary person!

Making a decision

Instead, a priest scratched out the question on a shell or bone, known as oracle bones. The oracle was then dripped with animal blood and heated until it cracked. The pattern of cracks contained Shangdi's answer. It could only be read by special priests called diviners. They announced whether Shangdi was for or against a decision, and the king acted on the advice.

An oracle shell from the Shang dynasty.

Secret power

Maybe Shangdi was really communicating with his people. Or maybe the shells cracked randomly. Who really knows? Because the king was the chief priest, he and the other priests stuck together. It was common in ancient societies for small groups to claim that only they could communicate with the gods. This gave them great power.

SO SHANGDI SAYS IT'S GOING TO RAIN LATER.

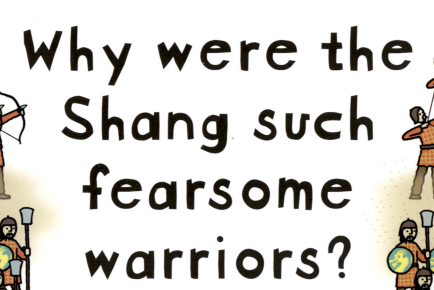

Why were the Shang such fearsome warriors?

The Shang dynasty came to power by defeating the Xia. They had to keep fighting to hold on to power.

Fighting the Fang

The Shang were surrounded by neighbours they called Fang, or barbarians. In other words, people who were inferior to the Shang. They got on with some groups of Fang. They disliked others. And with some the Shang switched between being friendly and going to war.

Everyone fall in

Would you want to be a Shang warrior? There wasn't much choice. Under most emperors, everyone was forced to join the army at times of war.

The Shang could put 13,000 warriors on the battlefield. For an ancient army, that was huge.

I HOPE THEIR AIM IS GOOD!

Close up or far away

The Shang army was divided into infantry and archers.

The infantry fought on foot close-up with the enemy. Their weapons were battle axes and bladed spears called halberds.

Archers had bows made from wood, bone and animal horn. The bows fired bronze-tipped arrows. A skilled archer could kill an enemy from 180 metres away. (Much safer than being in the infantry!)

Secret weapon

The Shang also had a secret weapon: **THE CHARIOT**. These two-wheeled vehicles were pulled by a pair of stocky horses attached to a long pole.

A driver steered the chariot while an archer fired at the enemy or struck at them with an axe or spear.

The chariot wasn't only used for warfare. It was also used for:

Ceremonies (they made kings feel important).

Punishments (they were used to tear criminals in two!).

Out of nowhere!

The Chinese often claim they invented the chariot. Experts disagree. They think the chariot design was copied from Central Asia. There are no traces of early types of chariot. So if the Chinese invented it, they got it right the first time. Which seems unlikely!

Why did the Shang bury things with the dead?

There's a famous saying: you can't take it with you. It means that all your stuff is no good when you're dead. Well, try telling that to the Shang!

The Shang buried their dead in tombs, surrounded by their favourite things.

Why all the stuff?

The Shang believed the dead went to the afterlife. In Shang beliefs, the afterlife was very like … er … the beforelife. Or daily life. The dead still needed to eat, look good, travel and even go shopping. So they needed their stuff buried with them.

So what did wealthy Shang take with them?

Cowrie shells

Jade

Bronze drinking vessels

WE NEIGH SIGNED UP FOR THIS!!

Horses, dogs and even servants!!

Chariots

What was it for?

Jars and cooking vessels were for preparing food. Cowrie shells were sometimes used as money, so they would help the dead to buy things. As for servants, they were sometimes killed so they could carry on working for their employers in the afterlife. Horses were killed to pull chariots.

The dogs were pets, for company.

WELL THAT'S OK THEN!

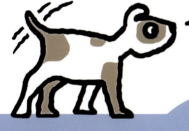

Big into bronze

Archaeologists love Shang graves. They learn a lot from the bones of the dead. They can learn even more from objects preserved in the tombs.

WOW!

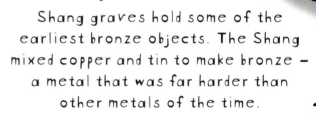

Shang graves hold some of the earliest bronze objects. The Shang mixed copper and tin to make bronze – a metal that was far harder than other metals of the time.

Egyptian tombs

It wasn't only the Shang who buried objects with the dead. The most famous grave goods are probably those buried with ancient Egyptians.

When the tomb of King Tutankhamun was opened in 1922, it contained 5,000 different treasures. There were chairs, games, ornaments, paintings and even model boats in case the dead king fancied a sail on the River Nile.

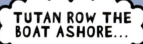

TUTAN ROW THE BOAT ASHORE...

What was so special about Fu Hao?

Women often got a bad deal in the ancient world. *(At least, that's how we see it today.)* **In most cultures, women did not have much power. They had to obey their father or husband. They weren't allowed to own their property or make their own decisions.**

 You have to admit, that seems VERY UNFAIR.

We don't know much about Shang women. Most information about them has been lost or destroyed. Historians guess they were treated as second-class citizens.

That was not always true, however. Meet … (drum roll please) …

Fu Hao!

Around 3,200 years ago, Fu Hao, or Lady Hao, was a queen of the Shang king Wu Ding. She wasn't the only one. Whenever Wu Ding made an alliance with one of the Shang's neighbours, he married a woman from that people.

First among equals

Wu Ding must have made a lot of alliances. Fu Hao was one of his 64 wives! Somehow, she made sure she was one of the most important. It helped that Fu Hao owned a lot of land. That meant she could give the king valuable presents, called tributes.

Fighting fit

Not only that. Fu Hao was also a warrior.

IS IT WIFE NUMBER 33 OR WIFE 52'S BIRTHDAY TODAY?

DON'T MESS WITH ME!

In fact, she was the greatest Shang general of her time!

This was her record in battle against the enemies of the Shang:

Battle	Result
Shang vs Tu-Fang	Win
Shang vs Yi	Win
Shang vs Qiang	Win
Shang vs Ba	Win

Grave robbery

When Fu Hao died, Wu Ding built her a large tomb away from the other royal Shang tombs. That helped protect it from grave robbers.

Just as well, because there was a lot to steal. Inside her grave, Fu Hao had 468 pieces of bronze, 564 pieces of bone, and 755 pieces of jade, 6,900 cowrie shells, six dogs – and 16 servants.

You can visit Fu Hao's tomb today, but almost all of the grave goods have been taken away and put in museums.

How did the Shang know what day it was?

The simple answer is that they looked at the night sky. They recorded the movements of the Sun, Moon and planets and used their observations to create a calendar.

THAT'S NEW!

The Moon changes appearance through a month.

A wonky calendar

The first Shang calendar depended on the Moon. Astronomers noticed that the Moon grows larger and smaller every 28 days.

However, a Moon-based calendar doesn't fit exactly with the length of a year. The calendar slips behind. Eventually, the calendar says it's summer, but it's snowing outside!

Solar, so good

A man named Wan-Nien used the Sun to work out that a year was 365 days long. (Today, we know it's actually 365¼ days long.) He also worked out the solstices. Those are the longest and shortest days of the year, which mark mid-summer and mid-winter, respectively.

The Sun always rises at the same place on the horizon on the longest day of the year, and on the shortest day. Using those dates, the Shang worked out a calendar of 12 months that each had 29 or 30 days. Once every seven years, they added an extra week to make sure the calendar remained correct.

WATCH ME RISE AND SET!

Ancient calendars

Calendars were important for all sorts of people in ancient society. Most people were farmers. They needed to know the best times for planting and harvesting.

Priests needed to know when to carry out different rituals to keep the gods happy.

Even generals needed to know the best times of year to go to war.

Were there dragons in China?

The answer to this question is easy: of course not! There are no such things as dragons, apart from in fairy tales – or maybe in fantasy shows on TV.

Decorative dragons

We know that now, but the Shang were not so sure. By the time of the Shang, the Chinese had been carving statues of dragons for centuries. Shang artists used dragons to decorate vessels and jewellery.

Dragon jewellery →

The Shang didn't see dragons as being harmful or dangerous. Shang dragons did not torment villagers or kidnap maidens. They didn't even breathe fire!

Dragon decorations

NOPE, JUST AIR.

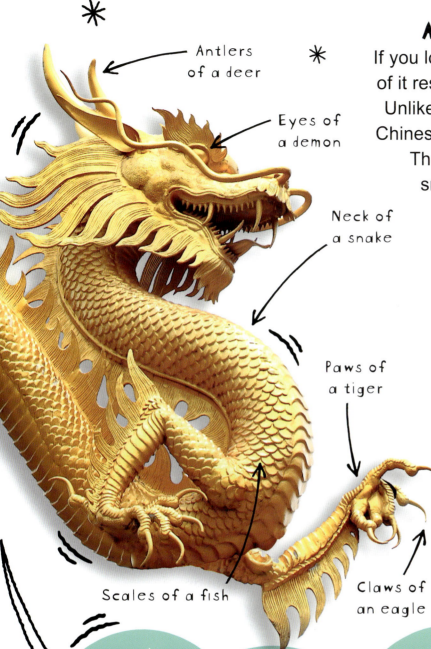

Antlers
of a deer

Eyes of
a demon

Neck of
a snake

Paws of
a tiger

Scales of a fish

Claws of
an eagle

An animal collection

If you look at a Chinese dragon, parts of it resemble bits of other creatures. Unlike dragons in Western Europe, Chinese dragons did not have wings. They were long and thin, like snakes, but with four legs.

Rare visitors

The Shang believed that in summer, Chinese dragons lived so high in the sky that no-one could see them. In winter, they lived deep below the oceans. They only visited the land rarely.

On those occasions, the dragons wanted to help people – not to burn them to ashes! Dragons could make it rain to help crops grow, for example.

Dragon country

Dragons remained important in Chinese culture long after the Shang. They are seen as strong and powerful. That reminded people of ... well, the king. (Woe betide anyone who didn't think the king was strong and powerful.)

So the dragon appeared on the king's robes and on imperial buildings. The imperial throne was called the Dragon Chair. The Chinese sometimes even call themselves 'descendants of the dragon'.

The 'Dragon Chair' in Beijing

Did the Shang invent writing?

No-one really knows who invented writing. For one thing, writing began in different parts of the world independently. In the Western world, writing began in ancient Sumer (now Iraq). In the Americas, it was probably started by the Olmec of Mesoamerica.

ON YOUR MARKS, GET SET... WRITE!

Chapter one

In China, the first writing that still survives is from about 1200 BCE, under the Shang. Written characters were carved on oracle bones (see pages 10-11) and bronze vessels. The hard objects helped the writing survive.

Lost for words

Shang characters were quite complex. That probably means that writing had begun earlier in China. Usually, it takes time for a writing system to stop being very simple. Perhaps this early writing was written on materials that have since rotted away.

We know that the Shang wrote on silk and bamboo. They both rot easily, so none of this writing survives (we know about it because later Chinese historians mention it).

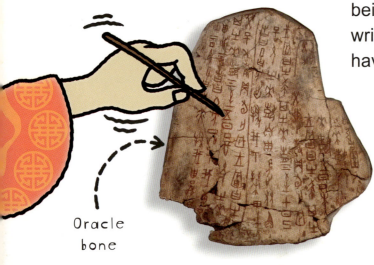

Oracle bone

So what did the Shang write about?

- Questions for the gods
- The gods' predictions of the future
- Records of the kings.

HEY, I WAS WRITING ON THAT!

Did you know?

The Shang were the first historical Chinese dynasty to leave any written records.

A Chinese scroll

Brought to book

Shang books were long rolls made by tying together thin strips of silk or bamboo. Each strip was a sentence or paragraph, written vertically from the top to the bottom. Chinese writing is still read from top to bottom.

After the fall of the Shang, the Zhou and the Qin continued to use their characters. That was how they became the basis of Chinese writing.

FOUR EYES ARE BETTER THAN TWO!

Clever Cangjie

According to Chinese legend, demons cried when humans invented writing because they knew that people could no longer be cheated.

In the legend, Chinese writing was invented by a historian named Cangjie in around 2650 BCE. He worked for China's legendary first ruler, the Yellow Emperor. Cangjie came up with a set of picture-like symbols – pictograms – based on animals, land forms and the patterns of the stars. Cangjie's four eyes were said to give him superhuman sight.

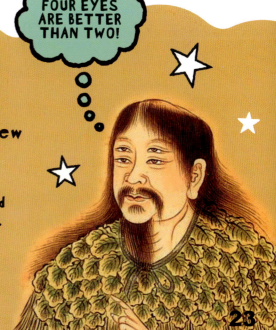

What was so special about green stone?

If you went to a Shang birthday party, what present should you take? There's only one answer: jade.

GREAT, MORE JADE!

The Shang loved jade.

Coloured stone

Jade is a semi-precious stone. It is most often green, but it also comes in other colours. The Shang's favourite jade was white. They called it mutton-fat jade.

As well as having beautiful colours, jade was also smooth and hard. Very hard. It had to be shaped by grinding it slowly with wet sand.

That. Took. Ages.

Jade objects were very expensive. That meant jade was a status symbol.

Symbolic stone

Jade was also symbolic. Peoples living before the Shang shaped circular jade disks with a hole in the middle to represent the sky. They were used as lucky charms.

Jade disk →

Jade never wore out, so the Shang saw it as a symbol of everlasting life. Later Chinese peoples made suits from jade in which to bury their dead. They hoped the jade would preserve the body for ever.

Beauty parade

The best-dressed Shang wore as much jade as they could afford: necklaces of jade beads, bracelets, rings, hair combs and earrings, as well as brooches, pendants and hooks to hang objects from belts.

Show-off Shang!

The Shang really cared about their appearance. They had mirrors of polished bronze to check themselves out. They pierced their ears, and wore their hair coiled up in a bun, held in place with carved bone hairpins. They dressed up in silk clothes, piled on their jade jewellery, and hey presto!

They were good to go.

CAN I GET ANY MORE JADE ON ME?

Why were moths so valuable?

What do you think of when you think of moths? Holes in your jumpers? Well, the Shang thought of luxury. They thought of super-light, super-smooth clothes woven from soft silk.

Why? Because silk comes from the silk moth.

MMMM YUMMY!

Silkworm caterpillars

Silky skills

Making silk was older than the Shang. The Chinese claim it was invented by Lady Hsi-Ling-Shih, wife of the legendary Yellow Emperor. She is said to have invented the loom for weaving silk.

In reality, no one knows who learned how to make silk. The Shang, though, perfected the process.

Weaving silk thread into cloth was traditionally a job for women.

Make your own silk

These are the steps they came up with:

① Feed caterpillars of the silk moth on mulberry leaves.

② Leave the caterpillars until they spin cocoons around themselves, ready to turn into pupae.

③ Take the cocoons and boil them in water. (Bye-bye, moths!)

④ When the cocoons are loose, unravel the fine fibres inside by hand.

⑤ When you have a bunch of long fibres, weave them together in threads of five or six.

⑥ Dye the threads whatever colours you want.

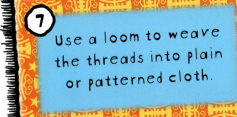

⑦ Use a loom to weave the threads into plain or patterned cloth.

As you can see, the process is long and complicated. It's also not very efficient. If you start out with 2,000 cocoons, you will end up with about 500 grams of silk.

That's not very much!

A rare material

The process also needs lots of workers. That makes it expensive (like jade). Only the royal family and other nobles could afford it. Later in Chinese history, non-royals were forbidden to wear silk by law.

Missing clothes

If you want to know what Shang clothes looked like... no-one actually knows. Silk might be very delicate, but that means it's also very ... er ... delicate. None has survived the last 3,000 years.

Quick-fire questions

Why was the Shang capital city of Yin Xu half-buried?

Ordinary Shang lived in homes that were dug into the ground and then covered with a roof. That provided lots of protection from the weather.

Why did the Shang feed the dead?

Everyone loves their families, right? Well, the Shang went one further. They offered food to their relatives who had died, because they believed that their spirits would help living members of the family. They sacrificed animals to them – and sometimes even humans! Ancestor worship still continues in parts of China (but not the human sacrifices!).

Was bronze worth more than gold?

Perhaps! It wasn't as shiny as gold, but it was far more useful. The Shang learned to make bronze by mixing 80 per cent copper with 20 per cent tin. Bronze was much stronger than copper. That made it great for forging farm tools and weapons – though most people couldn't afford it.

During Qingming festival, people visit the graves of their ancestors and leave them offerings.

Whose faces are on Shang cauldrons?

The Shang used bronze to make huge cauldrons called ding. Many ding are carved with taotie, which are fierce faces with protruding eyes. These creatures are part-human and part-animal. But apart from being able to tell that they are quite fierce, no-one knows what the taotie represent.

Did the royal family have sore ears?

The Shang court was full of music. It accompanied rituals and royal occasions. There were whole orchestras of instruments, such as bronze nao bells, cymbals and drums. There were also panpipes and flutes made out of bones. We know what the instruments sounded like, but we don't know what sort of music they played. Did it hurt people's ears? Well, that depends on how loudly the instruments were played!

Did the Shang really eat rhino?

GET ME OUT OF HERE!

Yes, rhino was sometimes on the Shang menu. Together with elephant and tiger. Their meat was cut into small pieces and fried or steamed, before being served with sweet or spicy sauces. (The Shang also ate more normal things, like fish, chicken, pig and deer.)

Glossary

Afterlife The place where people's souls are believed to live on after their death.

Alliance An association between countries that helps them both.

Ancestors Previous generations of a family.

Archaeologist Someone who studies physical remains of the past.

Bamboo A giant woody grass whose cane is used for many purposes.

Barbarian Someone who is considered uncivilised and inferior.

Calendar A chart or table that breaks the year into months and seasons.

Chariot A two-wheeled horse-drawn vehicle with a flat platform for a driver and passengers.

Cocoon A silky case spun by the larvae of many insects.

Cowrie shell The patterned, dome-shaped shell of a sea snail.

Exile The state of being banned from one's own country, usually as a punishment.

Grave goods Objects that are buried with a dead person.

Legendary Famous from ancient legends, or stories.

Loom A frame for weaving horizontal and vertical threads to make cloth.

Mandate of Heaven The idea that there was only one true ruler of China, who was permitted by the gods to overthrow false rulers.

Nutrients Chemicals that provide energy for plants or animals.

Oracle Someone who passes on advice from gods and goddesses to humans.

Pictograms Pictorial symbols that stand for words or phrases.

Prediction Forecast of what will happen in the future.

Ritual Solemn religious ceremony performed in a set way.

Sacrifice Something valuable that is offered as a gift to the gods.

Scroll A long roll of paper or other material for writing on.

Status symbol A possession that is a sign that someone is wealthy or important.

Vessel Hollow container that holds liquid or food.

Mini timeline

1600 BCE

Tang Cheng defeats the Xia and founds the Shang dynasty.

1200 BCE

Shang warriors begin to use chariots.

1401 BCE

King Pan Geng comes to the throne. He moves the Shang capital to Yin Xu.

1200 BCE

Fu Hao is buried in a tomb full of her possessions.

1250 BCE

The Shang begin to write on oracle bones.

1046 BCE

After a long period of decline, the last Shang king is overthrown by the neighbouring Zhou.

Further reading

Websites

www.bbc.co.uk/bitesize/clips/zsgj4j6

This BBC page has a video about how the Shang invented Chinese writing.

www.bbc.co.uk/bitesize/topics/z39j2hv

This page has an index of articles and videos about the Shang.

www.bbc.co.uk/bitesize/clips/z3s8g82

This video for students tells the story of the rise and fall of the Shang.

www.theschoolrun.com/homework-help/shang-dynasty

This site is intended to help students who are doing projects about the Shang.

www.twinkl.co.uk/blog/homework-help-the-shang-dynasty

This website has facts about the Shang, their beliefs and their military power.

Books

Great Empires: The Chinese Empire
by Ellis Roxburgh (Wayland, 2017)

Explore! Ancient China
by Izzi Howell (Wayland, 2016)

Great Civilisations: Shang Dynasty China
by Tracey Kelly (Franklin Watts, 2016)

The History Detective Investigates: The Shang Dynasty of Ancient China
by Geoffrey Barker (Wayland, 2015)

Index